GUIDE TO
GREAT BRITAIN

BRIAN WILLIAMS

Highlights for Children

Contents

On the cover: A sight-seeing boat passing under London's famous Tower Bridge, which spans the Thames River

Published by Highlights for Children
© 1995 Highlights for Children, Inc.

All rights reserved. No part of this book may be reproduced or transmitted in any form or by any means, electronic or mechanical, including photocopying, recording, or by any information storage and retrieval system, without permission in writing from the publisher.

10 9 8 7 6 5 4

ISBN 0-87534-915-3

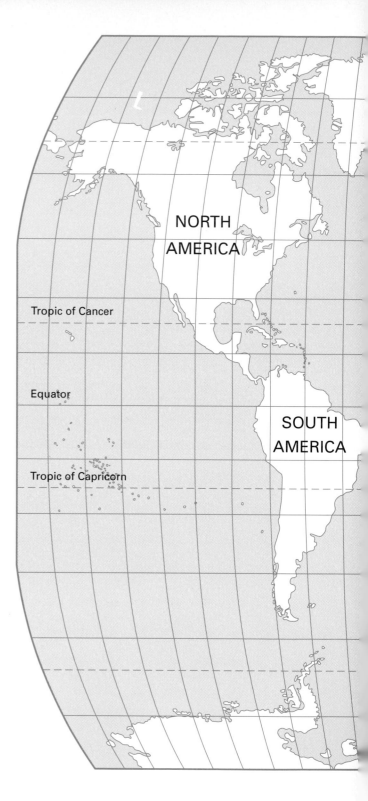

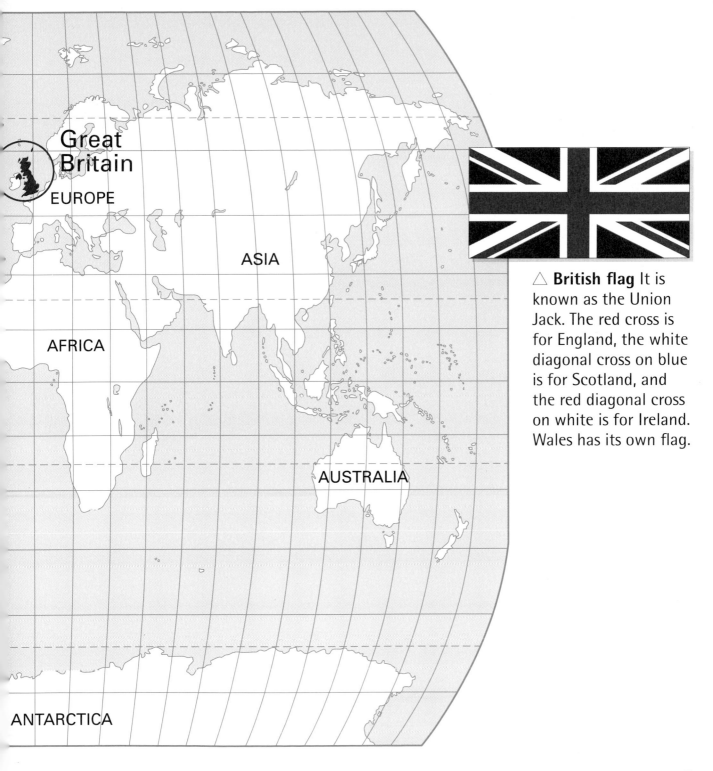

Great
Britain

EUROPE

ASIA

AFRICA

AUSTRALIA

ANTARCTICA

△ **British flag** It is known as the Union Jack. The red cross is for England, the white diagonal cross on blue is for Scotland, and the red diagonal cross on white is for Ireland. Wales has its own flag.

3

GREAT BRITAIN AT A GLANCE

Area 94,251 square miles (211,110 square kilometers)

Population 57,561,000

Capital London, population of city and surroundings is more than 6,500,000

Other big cities Birmingham (population 992,500), Glasgow (695,600), Leeds (711,700), Sheffield (509,000), Liverpool (455,600)

Highest mountain Ben Nevis in Scotland, 4,406 feet (1,343 meters)

Longest river Severn, 220 miles (354 kilometers)

Largest lake Loch Lomond in Scotland, 21 square miles (70 square kilometers)

Official language English

▽ **British stamps** All stamps in Great Britain have an image of Queen Elizabeth II's head on them. These stamps show industrial history, wildlife, and photographs of the queen.

◁ **British money** The currency of Great Britain is the pound. There are 100 pence in £1. On the front of a £10 note is a picture of Queen Elizabeth II. A scene from a cricket match and a portrait of the English writer Charles Dickens are on the back of the note.

10°W

5°W

0°

NORWAY

Orkney
Islands

Shetland
Islands

N
W   E
S

ATLANTIC
OCEAN

Outer Hebrides

Isle of
Skye

Loch
Ness   • Inverness

Cairngorms

The

• Aberdeen

▲ Ben Nevis

Highlands

SCOTLAND

North

Firth of Forth

Glasgow   Edinburgh

Clyde

Cheviot Hills   Newcastle

55°N

Sea

NORTHERN
IRELAND

Belfast

Tyne

Pennines

Tees

The Lake
District

Isle of
Man

Irish Sea

Blackpool

York

Bradford

REPUBLIC
OF
IRELAND

Dublin

Liverpool

Conway

Manchester

ENGLAND

The Wash

Caernarvon   ▲
Snowdon   Nottingham

Norwich

Severn

Birmingham

The Fens

WALES

Stratford
on Avon

Cambridge

Oxford

Swansea   Cardiff

Thames

London   ★

Canterbury

North Downs

Bristol

Bristol Channel

Winchester   South Downs

Dover

© Oxford Cartographers

Hastings

Southampton

Brighton

Exeter

Portsmouth

Dartmoor

Isle of Wight

50°N

Plymouth

English   Channel

FRANCE

BELGIUM

Channel Islands

GREAT BRITAIN

Farmland &
Woodland

Mountains

★ Capital

• Major Cities

▲ Mountain Peaks

— Country Boundary

0   25   50   75 Miles

0   50   100 Kilometers

 # WELCOME TO GREAT BRITAIN

Great Britain is an island nation. A narrow sea, the English Channel, divides it from France and the rest of Europe. The Atlantic Ocean lies between Great Britain and North America. Great Britain consists of England, Scotland, and Wales. With Northern Ireland — part of the island of Ireland — they form the United Kingdom. Being an island has been important in Britain's history and culture. It has encouraged British people to make strong links with other nations.

▽ **Portobello Market in London** You can buy almost anything from fruit to antique jewelry. Street markets are popular.

◁ **The game of bowls** Players roll large black balls at a small white target ball. People play bowls on neatly cut grass lawns in summer and indoors all year round.

The people of Great Britain are known as Britons, or the British. Most Britons also think of themselves as English, Scottish, or Welsh. Each place has its own traditions and history.

Great Britain is a surprisingly small nation. Three countries the size of Great Britain would fit into the state of Texas, with room to spare! Yet Britain has a great variety of scenery that ranges from flat farmland and gentle, rolling hills to beautiful lakes, highlands, and steep, rugged cliffs. There are no really high mountains. The climate is mild, with plenty of rainfall that makes fields and woods very green. Britain is a land of big cities and small villages. Crowded highways pass by quiet country lanes.

Most Britons live in the central and southern parts of the country. In the southeast corner is London, the capital city on the Thames River. London is big and busy. People of many different nationalities live and work, study, and trade in London's business district. Its main airport, Heathrow, is the world's busiest international airport. Visitors to Britain fly in from all over the world. Welcome to Britain.

◁ **The Lake District in northwest England** This is a region of hills, rivers, and lakes. Here busy towns seem far away.

HISTORIC LONDON

London, with its suburbs, is twice the size of New York City. Many Londoners live in the outer suburbs and travel into the city center by railroad, car, bus, or subway. Visitors driving in Britain find that traffic keeps to the left side of the road, not to the right as in the United States. Also, the steering wheels are on the right-hand side of vehicles.

▽ **Buses on Oxford Street** This is the busiest shopping street in London's West End.

The center of London is a mixture of tall office buildings, shops, and historic sites. A good way to explore the city is from the top deck of a London bus. You can also take the Underground, London's subway system, or ride in the distinctive black taxicabs.

London is never still or silent. By day, shoppers crowd the stores of Oxford Street and Regent Street. Many tourists visit the West End. It is the center of government and entertainment. Here you can tour royal buildings, shop in big stores, or visit a street market. Try feeding the pigeons in Trafalgar Square. In this big open area you can see Nelson's Column, a tall monument that honors British admiral Horatio Nelson.

At night, the West End theater district comes to life. People see plays in theaters around Piccadilly Circus. (Despite its name, it is not a circus with clowns and acrobats. It is a traffic circle.)

London has many other attractions. Walk through St. James's Park and watch ducks on the lake. Afterward join the crowd to see the Changing of the Guard outside Buckingham Palace, the London home of Queen Elizabeth II. London Zoo and the Open Air Theater are inside Regent's Park. In the British Museum are treasures such as the Rosetta Stone from Egypt, which helped scholars read ancient Egyptian writing. Madame Tussaud's is a museum that houses a magnificent collection of waxwork models.

◁ **A theater in the heart of the West End**
There are more than 40 theaters and hundreds of restaurants and snack bars within walking distance of each other.

▽ **Buckingham Palace** In front is a statue of Queen Victoria. She lived here in the late 1800s. Now the palace is home to her great-great-granddaughter, Queen Elizabeth II.

LONDON'S RIVER

The Thames is London's major river. The Houses of Parliament, location of the British legislature, or government, stand on its north bank at Westminster. Nearby is the 900-year-old church of Westminster Abbey, where famous Britons are buried. Riverboats travel east from Westminster to the City, the name for the oldest part of London.

▽ **St. Paul's Cathedral** It was built between 1675 and 1710 by Sir Christopher Wren.

The City is famous for Roman ruins, medieval churches and halls, modern offices, and hundreds of banks. Near the great dome of St. Paul's Cathedral lies Fleet Street, which became famous for its newspaper offices. An unusual landmark is Cleopatra's Needle. This 3,500-year-old stone monument was given to Britain by Egypt in 1819 — almost 1,900 years after Cleopatra's death.

Downriver is the Tower of London, where the British Crown Jewels are kept. In this medieval stone fortress, prisoners of the past had their heads cut off. Parts of the Tower are 900 years old. Tower Bridge stands alongside and looks just as old, but was only opened in 1894. The bridge's roadway can be raised to let tall ships pass.

Cargo ships packed London's docks when the City was the center of the British Empire. Now the docks district, renamed Docklands, is a business center. In the 1980s, many newspaper offices moved here from Fleet Street.

You can cruise downriver as far as Greenwich, where a king's palace once stood. The buildings you see today were opened as a hospital for sailors in the early 1700s. The National Maritime Museum, with its displays of historic ships, is close by. In Greenwich Park is the Observatory, founded in the 1600s to study the stars. The big clock here shows Greenwich Mean Time, by which the world checks its time.

◁ **A view over Greenwich**
From a hill in Greenwich Park, you can see the top of Canary Wharf Tower, Britain's tallest building, in Docklands.

▽ **Riverboats leaving and arriving at Westminster Pier**
From here, large boats carry passengers downriver to the Tower of London and on to Greenwich and upriver to Hampton Court royal palace.

COUNTRYSIDE AND COAST

Northeast of London is the flat farmland of Essex and East Anglia. Norwich, with its cathedral, is the largest city here. Southeast, across the Thames, is the county of Kent. This area, called the "Garden of England," is famous for fruit orchards and fields of hops, used to make beer.

▽ **The center of historic Canterbury** To the right in this view is Christ Church Gate, a medieval doorway to Canterbury Cathedral, which is more than 800 years old.

△ **Children in a school cooking class** Most children in Britain go to state-run schools.

▽ **A country pub** Pubs are very popular places for people to meet, drink, and have a snack or meal at lunchtime or in the evening.

In Kent you can visit Canterbury. In this ancient city, Saint Augustine, a missionary from Rome, taught the English about Christianity over 1,300 years ago. Take a walk around the city's medieval walls, and eat at one of the local inns. They have been used by travelers for hundreds of years.

Near Hastings, a small seaside town in Sussex, you can visit a historic battlefield. An army of Normans crossed the sea from France and landed here in 1066. Their leader, William, defeated the English in battle. He made himself king and changed England's history. Farther along the south coast are the famous white chalk cliffs of Dover and the entrance to the Channel Tunnel. This new undersea passage is popularly called the Chunnel. Travelers use it to cross between England and France on fast electric trains.

Southern England is the most crowded and wealthiest region of Britain. Its factories produce goods for shipment to Europe. From coastal towns such as Southend, thousands of people travel to work in London, using busy roads and railroads. Students use trains or buses to get to local schools and colleges.

Away from the towns lie quiet villages. Here, visitors should sample afternoon tea. A teashop will offer sandwiches, scones, cakes, and pots of tea. English people like drinking tea, but they like coffee, too. In summer, there are outdoor fairs, markets, farm shows, and cricket matches on village greens.

THE MIDLANDS AND THE NORTH

North of London is the region known as the Midlands. Birmingham, England's second largest city, is located here. Most buildings in its center are modern. Nearby Nottingham is famous for its medieval castle, lace, and for the deeds of the legendary outlaw, Robin Hood. In cities and towns, people live in neat rows of houses or in apartments.

The road north passes through the Peak District hills of Derbyshire. There are many small fields with sheep grazing, as well as beautiful stone cottages and churches. Here you can visit Hardwick Hall, Haddon Hall, and the majestic Chatsworth, one of the grandest houses in Britain.

Less than 300 miles (480 kilometers) from London is the "North of England." People living in this region think of London as being far away. Many of them never journey "down south." In Yorkshire, you see beautiful countryside and factory towns nestled in the valleys of the Pennine Hills. Industries involving coal, steel, and wool made towns such as Leeds, Bradford, and Sheffield grow rapidly. In York, you can listen to a cathedral choir and visit a Viking museum.

The big Humber and Tyne rivers flow eastward into the North Sea. The Humber Bridge is the longest single-span suspension bridge in the world—4,625 feet (1,410 meters). The North Sea fishing areas are busy with fishing boats from harbors on the east coast. The world's biggest ships were once launched from shipyards here. The shipyards have been replaced by automobile and electronics factories.

Oil and gas from offshore oilfields are piped ashore. Newcastle on Tyne is the biggest city of England's northeast region. From here, major roads lead north across the hills of Northumberland and over the English border to Scotland.

▷ **Chatsworth House** This huge estate with elegant gardens is the home of an English duke, but it is open to visitors.

▷ **The harbor at Whitby, Yorkshire** James Cook, explorer of the Pacific, was born here. The ruins of an abbey that was founded in 656 attract many visitors.

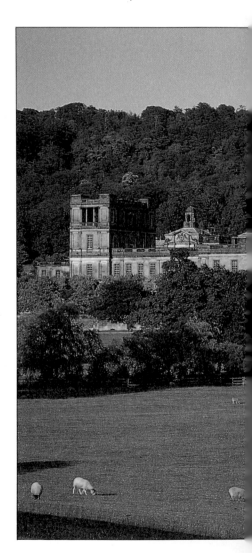

▽ **A car assembly plant** Britain builds automobiles in partnership with U.S., Japanese, and European companies.

INTO SCOTLAND

Scotland is a land of mountains, moors, rivers, lakes, and rugged coastline. For hundreds of years it had its own kings. Scotland's people, called Scots, continue to keep many of their own traditions.

Hills covered in rough grass and heather, known as the moors, are in the south of Scotland. Sheep and cattle roam the moors. Most Scots live in the cities and towns of the central lowlands. The two biggest cities are Glasgow and Edinburgh. Edinburgh, Scotland's capital, has a big arts festival every summer. Visitors walk along the main shopping street, Princes Street, and explore Edinburgh Castle. Inside the castle are the crown jewels of Scottish kings.

▷**John Knox's House**
This is one of the oldest houses in Edinburgh. It was the home of the spirited preacher, John Knox, who died in 1572. He was Scotland's most powerful religious and political leader.

▽ **Hadrian's Wall** This ancient structure divided Scotland and England. Named after a Roman emperor, the wall was built by Roman soldiers more than 1,800 years ago.

▽ **The Forth railroad bridge near Edinburgh** The steel bridge was built in the 1880s. Not far away, a modern suspension bridge spans the inlet, the Firth of Forth.

The Royal Mile leads from the castle to the palace of Holyrood House. Some of the buildings on this route date from the 1500s.

West of Edinburgh is Glasgow. Here many people are soccer fans. People meet in pubs, clubs, and coffee bars to discuss the Saturday or midweek game. Glasgow was once a great industrial city. It is now a cultural center with fine art galleries and museums. The city stands on Scotland's busiest river, the Clyde. The cruise ship, Queen Elizabeth II, was built here. Modern factories produce electronic goods.

Many of Scotland's rivers flow into the sea through long inlets called firths. Leaving Edinburgh, you cross the Firth of Forth by a road or railroad bridge. North and west of the Firth is the town of St. Andrews, home of the world's oldest golf club. The game has been played in Scotland since the 1500s.

HIGHLANDS AND ISLANDS

The Highlands of north Scotland have spectacular scenery. Visitors see rugged mountains, heather-covered *glens* (valleys), and sparkling *lochs* (lakes). Many lochs lie in the Great Glen (Glen More) between the towns of Inverness and Fort William. Ben Nevis, Britain's highest mountain, is south of the Glen. The biggest lake is Loch Lomond and the most famous is Loch Ness. Summer visitors to Loch Ness hope for a glimpse of the legendary Loch Ness Monster. It is popularly known as "Nessie."

The Highlands are the least populated parts of Britain. Here people live in small towns and villages. At the Highland Games, the Scots enjoy traditional sports, music, and folk dancing. The sports include "tossing the caber." (*Caber* is a Gaelic word for pole.) This is a competition to see who can throw a long, heavy wooden pole into the air and make it land closest to a target on the ground. Scottish bands play stirring tunes on the bagpipes and drums.

Deer roam the treeless moorland, where game birds called grouse are bred for hunting. Eagles are rare, but can be seen soaring in the sky. On some hills, forests have been planted for lumber. Dams on fast-flowing rivers make electricity. Oil and gas are pumped from oilfields beneath the sea off the northeast coast.

Many visitors think the most beautiful Scottish scenery is found on the islands to the west, the Hebrides. A boat will take you to the isles of Skye and Lewis. To the north are the Orkney and Shetland isles. Small farms here are called *crofts*. You will see longhorned Highland cattle and shepherds using collie dogs to round up the sheep.

▷ **A piper playing the bagpipes** He wears a tartan kilt, a short skirt worn by Scotsmen. To play the bagpipes, he uses his arm to force air out of a bag and through the pipes.

▷ **Urquart Castle on Loch Ness** People tell stories of a mysterious sea serpent living in this deep lake. But the Loch Ness "monster" is still only a legend.

LAKES AND SEASIDE

Long ago, England and Scotland were often at war. Raiders on horses would gallop south across the border into English cities like Carlisle. Some castles in this area are reminders of these times.

South of Carlisle is the Lake District. People enjoy camping, walking, climbing, fishing, and boating among its lakes and low mountains. One of the mountains, Scafell, is the highest in England at 3,209 feet (978 meters). The biggest lake is Windermere, which is 10½ miles (17 kilometers) long. Many visitors to the lakes drive a short distance north from the bustling towns of Merseyside and Lancashire. Liverpool and Manchester are the two biggest cities here.

◁ **Walkers above Ullswater** This is one of the lakes of the English Lake District. Poets and artists have praised the beauty of its scenery. This region is an English national park, looked after by rangers for the enjoyment of all.

▷ **Blackpool Tower** An iron tower 519 feet (158 meters) high overlooks sandy beaches and a long entertainment strip known as the "Golden Mile." A giant roller coaster 235 feet (71 meters) high can be found here.

▷ **Liverpool soccer fans** At a league match between Liverpool and Everton Football Clubs, fans wave flags and scarves in the colors of their teams.

Liverpool is a busy port at the mouth of the Mersey River. In the late 1700s cotton from the United States was sent by ship to Liverpool to be woven into cloth and then exported. Today, ferryboats regularly sail from Liverpool to Ireland and the Isle of Man. In the 1960s Liverpool became known for another reason. It is the hometown of the famous rock and roll band, the Beatles.

Sports fans come here to watch the annual Grand National horse race or soccer matches. Soccer is Britain's most popular game. Matches between neighboring city teams are supported by loyal, noisy fans.

Manchester grew as a trading center in the 1800s during Great Britain's industrial revolution. To escape work in mills and factories in northeast England, people took trips and vacations to the coast, or "seaside." Today, many Britons travel to sunny vacation spots all around the world. But Britain's most famous seaside resort of Blackpool still attracts crowds. They come to see its shows, theaters, and amusemement parks.

THE VALLEYS OF WALES

Just south of Liverpool is the border with Wales. The people of Wales are called Welsh, and many still speak the ancient Welsh language. In Wales you will see road signs and TV programs in both Welsh and English. In the Welsh language, the country is called *Cymru*, meaning "People of the valleys." Wales is smaller than Scotland or England and most of it is hilly. Most people in Wales live along the coasts or in small towns in the valleys of the south.

Wales and England share a long history. The huge stone castles of North Wales, such as those at Conwy and Caernarfon, were built by English kings. More than 450 years ago, the kings' soldiers defeated the Welsh in battle and joined the two countries. Even to this day the oldest son of Britain's king or queen has the title of Prince of Wales.

The port of Cardiff is the Welsh capital. It is a center for shopping, entertainment, business, sport, and culture. Its castle is a mixture of Roman fort, medieval stronghold, and 19th-century mansion.

The Welsh love singing. Music, poetry, and storytelling contests are held at the annual *eistedfodd*, or national festival. These contests can last for as long as a week.

Much of Wales is too hilly for growing crops. However, the land is used for raising sheep and for forestry. In the valleys, coal mines and slate quarries have been replaced by new factories making electronic products.

△ **Small cottages near an abandoned slate quarry** Slate is a gray rock. It used to be split into sheets and used for roofing houses. The workers, called quarrymen, lived close to their work.

Rugby union football is the Welsh national game. It is similar to American football. There are fifteen players on a rugby union team. Each year the national rugby union teams of Wales, Scotland, England, and Ireland compete with one another in a major championship.

◁ **A road sign in Welsh and English** Children in Wales are taught Welsh at school, but most people in Wales speak only English.

▽ **Pistyll Rhaedr waterfall** Wales has heavy rainfall and rivers fed by mountain lakes. Some of its fresh water is piped to England for drinking.

THE HEART OF ENGLAND

Fast trains speed from Cardiff to London in two hours. Road traffic leaving Wales for southwest England crosses a bridge over the Severn River, Britain's longest river. Bristol is the biggest city in England's southwest region. Merchants sailed from Bristol's port to the New World and Asia in the 1500s. Clifton Suspension Bridge near Bristol was built in 1864. It was designed by I. K. Brunel, who also designed steamships and railroads.

As you travel east, take time to visit the elegant city of Bath. For more than 1,500 years, people have come here for health cures, to drink the spa waters, and to bathe in warm springs. You can still see relics from the Roman baths built around A.D. 100.

Longleat House, a country estate, and Longleat Safari Park, a drive-through wildlife reserve, are set in the countryside in the nearby county of Wiltshire.

▽ **William Shakespeare's birthplace** The writer was born here in 1564.

▽ **Choristers of Magdalen College,** Oxford They are wearing the College uniform.

▽ **A canal lock** Canal boats shipped goods around Britain in the 1700s, but today canals are used mostly for pleasure boating.

Thousands of years ago, during the Stone Age, people built stone monuments all over southern England. Visitors to Avebury in Wiltshire marvel at the huge size of a stone circle that experts think was a meeting place. Not far away is another circle with its stones still standing. This is Stonehenge, England's most famous Stone Age site. It is more than 4,000 years old. The biggest stone here weighs 35 tons (36 tonnes).

Famous towns lie in the center of England. One is Oxford, where Britain's oldest university was founded in the 1100s. Another is Stratford upon Avon, where William Shakespeare was born. Visitors from all over the world come to the theater by the Avon River to see his plays. The cottage of his wife, Anne Hathaway, is another attraction. You can boat on canals and rivers to enjoy the sight of beautiful trees and meadows.

THE SOUTH COAST

You are never far from the sea in England. To the west, the land narrows toward Land's End in Cornwall. You can munch a Cornish pasty, a crisp pastry filled with meat and vegetables. In neighboring Devon, visit Plymouth, where the sailor Sir Francis Drake was born. The Pilgrims sailed to North America from this port in 1620.

In summer the south coast is popular for vacations. People who like old churches and cathedrals visit Winchester or Salisbury, where England's tallest cathedral spire is found. Those interested in ships go to Portsmouth, where two historic warships, the *Mary Rose* and the *Victory*, are preserved. Southampton is a port for cruise ships. Before jet planes became popular, ocean liners sailed from here to New York.

Inland is the New Forest with its wild ponies and trout streams. Brighton is a large coastal town. It has a Royal Pavilion built in Eastern style. You can hunt for souvenirs in the town's many antique shops.

If you are hungry, try some fish and chips, a traditional English meal. Or eat at one of the Indian and Chinese restaurants found in most towns in Britain. A summer treat is strawberries and cream. This dish is popular with tennis fans at Wimbledon during the All England Championships held in June. High above the tennis courts in south London, airplane passengers leaving Heathrow Airport have a last view of Britain.

△ **Children on a beach in Devon** Families enjoy seaside vacations, even if the sun does not shine every day of summer. Making sandcastles is fun.

▽ **A steam traction engine** Old working steam engines like this are displayed at fairs and carnivals. Such shows are a feature of British life in the summertime.

▽ **An old country church** Many village churches are several hundred years old. Both Britons and visitors enjoy exploring these buildings and learn more about Britain's past.

GREAT BRITAIN FACTS AND FIGURES

People

The people of Great Britain are mainly English, Scots, and Welsh. Other Britons include those whose ancestors came from other countries in Europe or from parts of the former British Empire. The Empire included India, Pakistan, Bangladesh, Canada, Australia, New Zealand, Kenya, Uganda, Jamaica, and Barbados.

Trade and Industry

Britain became a great trading and manufacturing nation in the 1800s. This was partly due to its large resources of coal and iron ore, but also to its great inventors. Britain produces enough oil and natural gas to meet its own needs from wells beneath the North Sea. About one-fifth of the country's energy comes from nuclear power.

Service industries, such as banks, insurance companies, and department stores, employ two-thirds of Britain's workers. London is Europe's major financial center. Britain's factories make machinery, vehicles, aerospace products, electronics, chemicals, textiles, clothing, and foods.

△ **A policeman outside 10 Downing Street** This is the main home and office of Britain's Prime Minister, the leader of the government.

Farming

Britain has well-run farms, but imports about a third of its food. Many farmers grow crops and raise animals. Important crops are barley, wheat, sugar beets, and potatoes. Sheep are the chief livestock, but dairy and beef cattle, hogs, and chickens are also raised.

Britain produces large amounts of milk, yogurt, cheese, butter, and eggs. Vegetables and fruit, especially potatoes, carrots, apples, pears, and raspberries, are grown.

Fishing

British fishing boats catch cod, haddock, herring, mackerel, flounder, and shellfish. The main fishing areas are in the North Sea and in the Atlantic Ocean. In Scotland especially, large amounts of freshwater fish such as salmon are caught or raised on fish farms.

Food

British people eat mostly meat, fish, eggs, and such vegetables as potatoes, beans, peas, and carrots. Lunch is often a snack, such as a sandwich and soup, or a hamburger or pizza from a fast-food restaurant.

People enjoy afternoon tea at about 4 P.M. when they drink tea (made in a teapot) and eat cake, sandwiches, or perhaps a scone with butter, jam, or cream.

Many people eat their main meal in the evening. French, Italian, Indian, Greek, and Chinese meals are very popular.

Traditional British dishes include:

fish and chips: fried fish and fried potatoes (french fries)

haggis: a Scottish dish made of ground meat, spices, oatmeal, and onion, boiled in a sheep's stomach

scone: round bread cooked on a griddle

steak and kidney pie: beefsteak and kidneys cooked in a pastry shell

Welsh rarebit: a dish of melted cheese on toast

Yorkshire pudding: a breadlike side dish often served with roast beef

Schools

Education in state schools is free, but some parents pay for their children to go to private schools. All British children must go to school from the age of 5 to 16. Some attend preschool nurseries or playgroups. From ages 5 to 11 children attend elementary school. They go on to secondary school. About a third of pupils continue into higher education after age 18.

There are more than seventy universities in Britain. The oldest are Oxford and Cambridge. There are also many specialized colleges.

△ **The futuristic-looking Lloyd's Building**
In 1688 Lloyd's of London was established by British merchants to insure goods carried at sea.

The Media

The British Broadcasting Corporation (BBC) broadcasts television and radio programs. Private broadcasting corporations provide regional TV networks and commercial radio. British viewers can also receive satellite and cable television programs.

Britain has more than 100 daily newspapers. The biggest-selling national newspaper is *The Sun*, with more than three million readers every weekday. The most famous is *The Times*. It was first published in 1785. There are also many regional newspapers, such as *The Scotsman*, and hundreds of magazines for both adults and children. Comics, with strip cartoons, are also popular with children.

Art and Drama

Britain has a rich artistic tradition, with many influences from the rest of Europe. British painters are noted for landscapes and portraits. They include Thomas Gainsborough, Joseph Turner, and John Constable.

Drama has been popular and important since the 1500s, when William Shakespeare wrote his many plays. In more recent times, movie films and photography are popular.

There are excellent British ballet, modern dance, and opera companies, and a fine tradition of orchestral and choral music. Folksong and pop music in various styles also flourish.

GREAT BRITAIN FACTS AND FIGURES

Literature

The books of Jane Austen and Charles Dickens are world famous. So are the stories about the detective Sherlock Holmes written by Arthur Conan Doyle.

English poetry dates from the 700s, when the English language was very different from modern English. Famous poets in English include Geoffrey Chaucer, John Keats, and William Wordsworth. Scotland's best-known poet is Robert Burns.

△ **A soldier stands guard at Windsor Castle**
This castle, west of London, is one of the homes of the British royal family. Red uniforms are worn for ceremonial duty only.

Religion

Most people in Britain are Protestant. The Queen is named Head of the Church of England, but its leader is the Archbishop of Canterbury. There are also more than five million Roman Catholics, about a million Muslims, and about half a million British Jews.

Festivals and Holidays

Britain has few national or religious holidays compared with other countries. Here are a few:
January 1 **New Year's Day** On New Year's Eve (the night before) people "first foot," to visit neighbors and welcome in the New Year. In Scotland, New Year is known as Hogmanay, and January 2 is a holiday.

March 1 **St. David's Day** Although not an official holiday, it is a celebration of the patron saint of Wales.
April 23 **St. George's Day** is the festival of the patron saint of England. It, too, is not an official holiday.
Bank Holidays These include Good Friday, Easter Monday, Christmas Day, and Boxing Day (December 26). They are called bank holidays because originally government offices and banks closed on those days. There are also spring and summer bank holidays on the last Monday in May and August.
November 30 **St Andrew's Day** is celebrated in Scotland, though it is not an official holiday.

Plants

Few of Britain's original forests remain. In the woodland that exists, oak, beech, and ash are typical trees. Scotland has treeless moorland, peatbogs, and pine forests.

Parks and public gardens are a feature of many towns. Many British people also take pride in their own flower and vegetable gardens.

Animals

The biggest wild animals are red deer and small moorland ponies. Foxes are common, even in towns. Other mammals include badgers, otters, rabbits, and gray squirrels. Britain has few reptiles because of its chilly climate, but is rich in birdlife and freshwater fish.

Sport

The British invented a number of the world's major sports, including soccer, cricket, rugby, and golf. Soccer, or football, is the nation's most popular sport. Rugby football is especially popular in Wales.

Cricket is the main summer game in England. Britain's popular sports and recreational activities include field hockey, track and field, tennis, golf, fishing, horse riding, climbing, and sailing.

HISTORY

The earliest inhabitants of Britain were Stone Age hunters who lived more than 500,000 years ago. About 6,000 years ago, settlers from the continent of Europe cleared forests and began farming. The Celts from Central Europe brought the first iron tools about 3,000 years ago.

Britain was invaded by the Romans in A.D. 43 and by Anglo-Saxons (from Germany) and Vikings (from Scandinavia) from the 500s onward. In 1066, the Normans from France conquered England. By the end of the Middle Ages (about 1450), England had conquered Wales, and by 1500 England also ruled Ireland.

Gradually the king's power was challenged by nobles and by merchants. Parliament gained power, and this was the beginning of democracy. England and Scotland were united under one king from 1603. In the 1640s there was a civil war between the king's and parliament's forces. Parliament's forces won, and though Britain still has a queen today, Elizabeth II has no real power in government.

By the 1700s Britain had a growing overseas empire. The United States broke away in 1776, but Canada, India, Australia, and large areas in Africa came under British control. The industrial revolution of the late 1700s and 1800s made Britain wealthy, and by 1900 Britain ruled the largest empire ever seen. But the two world wars weakened its power and its empire broke up. Since 1973 Britain has been a member of the Common Market, now the European Union, a trading union of the major European nations.

LANGUAGE

English is spoken throughout Great Britain, but there are regional variations, or dialects. People may use different words for the same thing. Some people in Wales speak Welsh, and some Scots speak Gaelic. These are forms of ancient Celtic languages. Immigrants from Asia speak languages such as Urdu as well as English. British English uses some different words from American English. Here are a few common, and some unusual, examples.

American	British
hurry or run after	beetle off
trunk (of a car)	boot
a derby hat	bowler
umbrella	brolly
good-bye	cheerio
a receipt or piece of paper	chit
nonsense	codswallop
potato chips	crisps
apartment	flat
television set	goggle box
a bag or suitcase	holdall

American	British
elevator	lift
truck	lorry
friend or buddy	mate
expressway or freeway	motorway
bill (money)	note
an old car	an old banger
sidewalk	pavement
gasoline	petrol
garbage, trash	rubbish
a difficult situation	a sticky wicket
subway	underground

INDEX

Acknowledgments
Book created for Highlights for Children, Inc. by Bender Richardson White.
Editor: Lionel Bender
Designer and page make-up: Malcolm Smythe
Art Editor: Ben White
Editorial Assistant: Madeleine Samuel
Picture Researcher: Madeleine Samuel
Production: Kim Richardson

Maps produced by Oxford Cartographers, England.
Banknotes from Thomas Cook Currency Services.
Stamps from Stanley Gibbons.

Editorial Consultant: Andrew Gutelle
Guide to Great Britain is approved by the British Tourist Authority, London
Great Britain Consultant: David Marshall, Educational Publishing Consultant
Managing Editor, Highlights New Products: Margie Hayes Richmond

Picture Credits
EU = Eye Ubiquitous, Z = Zefa.
t = top, b = bottom, l = left, r = right.
Cover: Z. Pages: 6-7: Z. 7t: Z/B. Benjamin 8: Z. 9t: EU/Tony Brown.9b: EU/Paul Thompson. 10: Z. 11t: EU/Julia Waterlow. 11b: Z/R. Nicholas. 12: Z. 13t: Alexander McIntyre. 13b: Z. 14-15: EU. 15t: EU.15r: Nissan Car Company. 16b: Lionheart Books. 16-17: Z. 17: Z. 18: EU/Paul Thompson.19t, 19b: Z. 20: Z/W. F. Davidson. 21l: EU/Paul Thompson. 21r: EU/Steve Lewis. 22: Z. 23t: EU/Davy Bold. 23b: Z. 24l: Z. 24r: Alexander McIntyre. 25: Z. 26t: Lionheart Books. 26b, 27: Alexander McIntyre. 28: Z. 29: EU/P. W. Hutley. 30: Z.